Charles Manson

Helter Skelter and Beyond

Filiquarian Publishing, LLC.

Charles Manson: Helter Skelter and Beyond is available for free download at
www.biographiq.com/bookd/H971

Filiquarian Publishing, LLC.

Charles Manson

Helter Skelter and Beyond

Charles Milles Manson (b. November 12, 1934) is a convict who led the "Manson Family," a quasi-commune that arose in the U.S. state of California in the later 1960s.[1][2][3] He was found guilty of conspiracy to commit the Tate-LaBianca murders, which members of the group carried out at his instruction. Through the joint-responsibility rule of conspiracy,[4] he was convicted of the murders themselves.

Manson is forever associated with "Helter Skelter," the term he took from the Beatles song of that name and construed as a race-based conflict that the crimes were intended to precipitate. This unusual connection with rock music linked him, from the beginning of his notoriety, with pop culture, in which he became a symbol of transgression, rebellion, evil, ghoulishness, bloody violence, homicidal psychosis, and the macabre. Ultimately, the term was used as the title of the book that prosecutor Vincent Bugliosi wrote about the Manson murders.

At the time the Family began to form, Manson was an unemployed ex-convict, who had spent half his life in correctional institutions for a variety of offenses. In the period before the murders, he was a distant fringe member of the Los Angeles music industry, chiefly via a chance association with Beach Boy Dennis Wilson. After Manson was charged with the crimes, recordings of songs written and performed by him were released commercially; a number of artists have covered his songs in the decades since.

Manson's death sentence was automatically reduced to life imprisonment when a decision by the Supreme Court of California temporarily eliminated the state's death penalty.[5] California's eventual reestablishment of capital punishment did not affect Manson, who is an inmate at Corcoran State Prison.

Early Life

Childhood

First known as "no name Maddox,"[6][7][8] Manson was born to the unmarried Kathleen Maddox in Cincinnati General Hospital, Cincinnati, Ohio; no more than three weeks after his birth, he was Charles Milles Maddox.[6][9][10] For a period, after her son's birth, Kathleen Maddox was married to a laborer named William Manson,[10] whose last name the boy was given. Charles Manson's biological father appears to have been a "Colonel Scott," against whom Maddox filed a bastardy suit that resulted in an agreed judgment in 1937.[6] Possibly, Charles never really knew him.[6][8]

Young Manson's mother, allegedly a drinker,[6] once sold him for a pitcher of beer to a childless waitress, from whom his uncle retrieved him some days later.[7] When his mother and her brother were sentenced to five years imprisonment for robbing a service station in 1939, Manson was placed in the West Virginia home of an aunt and uncle who were very religious. Upon his mother's 1942 parole, Manson was returned to his mother and lived with her in run-down hotel rooms.[6]

In 1947, Kathleen Maddox tried to have her son placed in a foster home but failed because no such home was available.[6] The court placed Manson in Gibault School for Boys, Terre Haute, Indiana. After ten months, he fled from there to his mother, who rejected him.[6]

First Offenses

By burglarizing a grocery store, Manson obtained cash that enabled him to rent a room.[6] A string of burglaries of other stores, from one of which he stole a bicycle, ended when he was caught in the act and sent to an Indianapolis juvenile center. His escape after one day led to his recapture and his placement in Boys Town, from which he escaped with another boy four days after his arrival. The pair committed two armed robberies on their way to the home of the other boy's uncle.[11]

Caught during the second of two subsequent break-ins of grocery stores, Manson was sent to the Indiana School for Boys at age thirteen. After many failed attempts, he escaped with two other boys in 1951. In Utah, having burglarized gas stations all along the way, the three were caught driving to California in cars they had stolen. For the federal crime of taking a stolen car across a state line, Manson was sent to the Washington, D.C., National Training School for Boys. Despite four years of schooling and an average IQ of 109 (later tested at 121),[11] he was illiterate. A caseworker concluded he was aggressively antisocial.[11]

First Imprisonment

Less than a month before a scheduled February 1952 parole hearing at Natural Bridge Honor Camp, a minimum security institution to which he had been transferred the previous October on a psychiatrist's recommendation, Manson "took a razor blade and held it against another boy's throat while he sodomized him."[11][7] He was transferred to the Federal Reformatory, Petersburg, Virginia, where he was considered "dangerous."[11] In September 1952, a number of other serious disciplinary offenses resulted in

Manson's transfer to the Federal Reformatory at Chillicothe, Ohio, a more secure institution.[11]

About a month after the transfer, Manson became almost a model resident. Good work habits and a rise in his educational level from the lower fourth to the upper seventh grade won him a May 1954 parole.[11]

After temporarily honoring a parole condition that he live with his aunt and uncle in West Virginia, Manson moved in with his mother in that same state. In January 1955, he married Rosalie Jean Willis, a hospital waitress, and made a living with smalltime jobs and stealing cars. Around October, about three months after he and his pregnant wife arrived in Los Angeles in a car he had stolen in Ohio, he was again charged with a federal crime; after a psychiatric evaluation, he was given five years' probation. His subsequent failure to appear at a Los Angeles hearing on an identical charge filed in Florida resulted in his March 1956 arrest in Indianapolis. His probation was revoked; he was sentenced to three years' imprisonment at Terminal Island, San Pedro, California.[11]

Charles Manson Jr., Manson's son by Rosalie, was born while Manson was in prison. During his first year at Terminal Island, Manson received visits from his wife and mother, who were now living together in Los Angeles; but in March 1957, when the visits from his wife ceased, his mother informed him Rosalie was living with another man. Caught trying to escape by stealing a car less than two weeks before a scheduled parole hearing, Manson was given five years' probation; his parole was denied.[11]

Second Imprisonment

Manson received five years parole in September 1958, the same year in which Rosalie received a decree of divorce. By November, he was pimping a sixteen-year-old girl and was receiving additional support from a girl with wealthy parents. Pleading guilty in September 1959 to a charge of attempting to cash a forged U.S. Treasury check, he received a ten-year suspended sentence and probation after a young woman with an arrest record for prostitution tearfully told the court she and Manson were in love and would marry if Manson were freed.[11]

After Manson took that same woman and another girl from California to New Mexico for purposes of prostitution before the year's end, he was held and questioned for violation of the Mann Act. Though he was released, he evidently suspected, rightly, that the investigation had not ended. When he disappeared, in violation of his probation, a bench warrant was issued; an April 1960 indictment for violation of the Mann Act followed.[11] Arrested in Laredo, Texas, in June, when one of his girls was arrested for prostitution, Manson was returned to Los Angeles. For violation of his probation on the check-cashing charge, he was ordered to serve his ten-year sentence.[11]

In July 1961, after a year spent unsuccessfully appealing the revocation of his probation, Manson was transferred from the Los Angeles County Jail to the United States Penitentiary at McNeil Island, Washington. Although the Mann Act charge had been dropped, the attempt to cash the Treasury check was still a federal offense. His September 1961 annual review noted he had a "tremendous drive to call attention to himself," an observation echoed in September 1964.[11]

In June 1966, Manson was sent, for the second time in his life, to Terminal Island, in preparation for early release. By March 21, 1967, his release day, he had spent more than half of his thirty-two years in prisons and other institutions.[11] Telling the authorities that prison had become his home, he requested, unsuccessfully, that he be permitted to stay,[11] a fact touched on in a 1981 television interview:

Tom Snyder: Let's go back to 1967, the time you were winding up serving a term of a number of years, ten years, and written accounts indicate that you told the authorities, "Don't let me out, I can't cope with the outside world." Do you have a recollection of that? And do you –

Manson: You're making a desperate plea out of something, man. There's no desperate plea out of it. I said I can't handle the maniacs outside, let me back in.

Snyder: I didn't use the word desperate; that's your word, Charles.

Manson: Yeah, well, your inflection and your voice tones were, uh, implications there.[12]

Rise of the Family

On his release day, Manson requested and was granted permission to move to San Francisco, where, with the help of a prison acquaintance, he obtained an apartment in Berkeley. In prison, he had been taught to play steel guitar by 1930s bank robber Alvin Karpis;[11][13][7] now, living mostly by panhandling, he soon got to know Mary Brunner, a twenty-three-year-old University of Wisconsin-Madison graduate working as an assistant librarian at UC Berkeley. After moving in with her, he overcame her resistance to his bringing other women in to live with them. Before long, they were sharing Brunner's residence with eighteen other women.[14]

Manson also established himself as a guru in San Francisco's Haight-Ashbury, which, during 1967's Summer of Love, was emerging as the signature hippie locale. Expounding a philosophy that included some of the Scientology he had studied in prison,[15] he soon had his first group of young followers, most of them female.[11]

Before the summer was out, Manson and eight or nine of his enthusiasts piled into an old school bus they had re-wrought in hippie style, with colored rugs and pillows in place of the many seats they had removed. Hitting the road, they roamed as far north as Washington State, then southward through Los Angeles, Mexico, and the southwest. Returning to the Los Angeles area, they lived in Topanga Canyon, Malibu, and Venice — western parts of the city and county.[14]

In an alternative account, which included no mention of the eighteen girls at Brunner's place, Manson, apparently accompanied by Brunner, acquired Family members during some months of travels that were undertaken, in part, in a Volkswagen van; it was November when the school bus set out from San Francisco with the enlarged group.[16]

Involvement with Wilson, Melcher, et al.

The events that would culminate in the murders were set in motion in late spring 1968, when, by some accounts, Dennis Wilson, of The Beach Boys, picked up two hitchhiking Manson girls and brought them to his Pacific Palisades house for a few hours. Returning home in the early hours of the following morning from a night recording session, Wilson was greeted in the driveway of his own residence by Manson, who emerged from the house. Uncomfortable, Wilson asked the stranger whether he intended to hurt him. Assuring him he had no such intent, Manson began kissing Wilson's feet.[17][18] (According to the quasi-autobiographical Manson in His Own Words, Manson first met Wilson at a friend's San Francisco house where he, Manson, had gone to obtain marijuana. The Beach Boy supposedly gave Manson his Sunset Boulevard address and invited him to stop by when he would be in Los Angeles.)[7]

Inside the house, Wilson discovered twelve strangers, mostly girls.[17][18] Over the next few months, as their number doubled, the Family members who had made themselves part of Wilson's Sunset Boulevard household cost him approximately $100,000. This included a large medical bill for treatment of their gonorrhea and $21,000 for the accidental destruction of an uninsured car of his they borrowed.[19] Wilson would sing and talk with Manson, whose girls were servants to them both.[17]

Wilson paid for studio time to record songs written and performed by Manson and introduced Manson to acquaintances of his with roles in the entertainment business. These included Gregg Jakobson, Terry Melcher, and Rudi Altobelli.[17] Jakobson, who was impressed by "the whole Charlie Manson package" of artist/lifestylist/philosopher, also paid to record Manson material.[20][21][22][23]

Spahn Ranch

By August 1968, when Wilson had his manager clear the Family members from his house, Manson had established a base for the group at Spahn's Movie Ranch, not far from Topanga

Canyon.[24][25] The evictees joined the rest of the Family there.[17]

Located in (or near) Chatsworth, the ranch had once been a location for the shooting of Western films; then, with its old movie sets run down, it was primarily doing business in horseback rides. While Family members did helpful work around the place, Manson kept the nearly-blind, octogenarian owner, George Spahn, on his side by having Lynette Fromme act as Spahn's eyes and, along with other girls, attend to Spahn sexually.[26][27] For a tiny squeal she would emit when Spahn would pinch her thigh, Fromme, one of the early Family members who had boarded the school bus,[14] won from Spahn the nickname "Squeaky."[19]

The Family was soon joined at Spahn Ranch by Charles Watson, who had met Manson at Dennis Wilson's house. A small-town Texan who had quit college and moved to California,[28] Watson had given a lift to Wilson, who had been hitchhiking because his cars had been wrecked.[24] Watson's drawl earned him, too, a George Spahn nickname, "Tex."[25]

Helter Skelter

In the first days of November 1968, Manson established the Family at alternate headquarters in Death Valley's environs, where they occupied two unused (or little-used) ranches, Myers and Barker.[23][29] The former, to which the group had initially headed, was owned by the grandmother of a new girl in the Family. The latter was owned by an elderly, local woman to whom Manson presented himself and a male Family member as musicians in need of a place congenial to their work. When the woman agreed to let them stay there if they'd fix up things, Manson honored her with one of the Beach Boys' gold records,[29] several of which he'd been given by Dennis Wilson.[30]

While back at Spahn Ranch, no later than December, Manson and Tex Watson visited a Topanga Canyon acquaintance who played them the Beatles' White Album, then recently released.[23][31][32] Despite having been twenty-nine years old and imprisoned when The Beatles first came to America, in 1964, Manson had been all but obsessed with the group. At McNeil, he had told fellow inmates, including Alvin Karpis, that he could surpass the group in fame;[11][33] to the Family, he spoke of the group as "the soul" and "part of 'the hole in the infinite.'"[32]

For some time, too, Manson had been saying that racial tension between blacks and whites was growing and that blacks would soon rise up in rebellion in America's cities.[34][35] He had emphasized Martin Luther King, Jr.'s assassination, which had taken place on 4 April 1968.[29] On a bitter cold New Year's Eve at Myers Ranch, the Family members, gathered outside around a large fire, listened as Manson explained that the social turmoil he had been predicting had also been predicted by The Beatles.[32] The White Album songs, he declared, told it all, although in code. In fact, he maintained, the album was directed at the Family itself, an elect group that was being instructed to preserve the worthy from the impending disaster.[34][35]

In early January 1969, the Family escaped the desert's cold by establishing yet another base, at a canary-yellow home in Canoga Park, not far from

the Spahn Ranch. Because this locale would allow
the Family to remain "submerged beneath the
awareness of the outside world,"[36][37] Manson
called it the Yellow Submarine, another Beatles
reference. There, the group prepared for the
impending apocalypse, which, around the
campfire, Manson had termed "Helter Skelter,"
after the White Album song of that name.

By February, Manson's vision was complete. The
Family would create an album whose songs, as
subtle as those of The Beatles, would trigger the
predicted chaos. Ghastly murders of whites by
blacks would be met with retaliation, and a split
between racist and non-racist whites would yield
whites' self-annihilation. Blacks' triumph, as it
were, would merely precede their being ruled by
the Family, which would ride out the conflict in
"the bottomless pit" — a secret city beneath Death
Valley.[38] At the Canoga Park house, while
Family members worked on vehicles and pored
over maps to prepare for their desert escape, they
also worked on songs for their world-changing
album. When they were told Terry Melcher was to
come to the house to hear the material, the girls

prepared a meal and cleaned the place; but Melcher never arrived.

Encounter with Tate

On March 23, 1969,[39] Manson entered uninvited upon 10050 Cielo Drive, which he had known as the residence of Terry Melcher.[20] By that time Melcher was no longer residing there. Since that February,[40] the tenants had been actress Sharon Tate and her husband, director Roman Polanski.

Manson was met by Shahrokh Hatami, a photographer and Tate friend, who was there to photograph Tate in advance of her departure for Rome the next day. Having seen Manson through a window as Manson approached the main house, Hatami had gone onto the front porch to ask him what he wanted.[39]

When Manson told Hatami he was looking for someone whose name Hatami did not recognize, Hatami informed him the place was the Polanski residence. Hatami advised him to try "the back alley," by which he meant the path to the guest house, beyond the main house.[39]

Concerned over the stranger on the property, Hatami was now down on the front walk, to confront Manson. When Tate appeared behind Hatami, in the house's front door, and asked who was calling, Hatami said a man was looking for someone. Hatami and Tate maintained their positions while Manson, without a word, went back to the guest house, returned a minute or two later, and left.[39]

That evening, Manson returned to the property and again went back to the guest house, where, presuming to enter the enclosed porch, he spoke with Rudi Altobelli, who was just coming out of the shower. Although Manson asked for Melcher, Altobelli, who owned the property and had leased it to Melcher and then the Polanskis, felt Manson had come looking for him.[41] (Los Angeles Deputy District Attorney Vincent Bugliosi, who would eventually prosecute Manson, obtained information that suggested Manson had been to the place on earlier occasions since Melcher's departure from it.)[39][42]

Speaking through the inner screen door, Altobelli told Manson that Melcher had moved to Malibu; he lied that he did not know Melcher's new address. In response to a question from Manson, Altobelli said he himself was in the entertainment business, although, having met Manson the previous year, at Dennis Wilson's home, he was sure Manson already knew that. At Wilson's, Altobelli had complimented Manson lukewarmly on some of his musical recordings that Wilson had been playing.[39]

When Altobelli informed Manson he was going out of the country the next day, Manson said he'd like to speak with him upon his return; Altobelli lied that he would be gone for more than a year. In response to a direct question from Altobelli, Manson explained that he had been directed to the guest house by the persons in the main house; Altobelli expressed the wish that Manson not disturb his tenants.[39]

Manson left. As Altobelli flew with Tate to Rome the next day, Tate asked him whether "that creepy-looking guy" had gone back to the guest house the day before.[39]

Family Crimes

Crowe Shooting; Hinman Murder

By June, Manson was telling the Family they might have to show blacks how to start Helter Skelter.[36][43][44] When Manson tasked Tex Watson to obtain money supposedly intended to help the Family prepare for the conflict, Watson defrauded a black drug dealer named Bernard "Lotsapoppa" Crowe; Crowe responded with a threat to wipe out everyone at Spahn Ranch. Manson countered on July 1, 1969, by shooting Crowe at his Hollywood apartment.[45][46][26][47]

Manson's mistaken belief that he had killed Crowe was seemingly confirmed by a news report of the discovery of the dumped body of a Black Panther in Los Angeles. Although Crowe was not a member of the Black Panthers, Manson, concluding he had been, expected retaliation from the group. He turned Spahn Ranch into a defensive camp, with night patrols of armed guards.[45][48]

On July 25, 1969, Manson sent sometime Family member Bobby Beausoleil along with Mary Brunner and Family member Susan Atkins to the house of acquaintance Gary Hinman, to persuade him to turn over money Manson thought Hinman had inherited.[49][45][50] (In a 1981 Oui magazine interview[51] and 1998-99 Seconds magazine interviews,[52] Beausoleil said he went to Hinman's house to recover money paid to Hinman for drugs that had turned out to be bad. He said Brunner and Atkins, unaware of his purpose, went with him idly, to visit Hinman.)

The three held the uncooperative Hinman hostage for two days, during which Manson showed up with a sword to slash his ear. After that, Beausoleil stabbed him to death, ostensibly on Manson's instruction. Before leaving the Topanga Canyon residence, Beausoleil, or one of the girls, used Hinman's blood to write "Political piggy" on the wall and to draw a panther paw, a Black Panther symbol.[46][26][53]

On August 6, Beausoleil was arrested after he was caught driving Hinman's car, whose tire well held the murder weapon.[40] On August 8, 1969, Manson told Family members at Spahn Ranch, "Now is the time for Helter Skelter."[54][55][45]

Tate Murders

On the night of August 8, 1969, Manson directed Tex Watson to take Family members Atkins, Linda Kasabian, and Patricia Krenwinkel — one of the hitchhikers allegedly picked up by Dennis Wilson[17] — to "that house where Melcher used to live" and "totally destroy everyone in [it], as gruesome as you can."[56][57] He told the girls to do as Tex would instruct them.[54][58]

When the four arrived at the entrance to the Cielo Drive property, Watson, who'd been to the house, on Family business,[23] climbed a telephone pole near the gate and cut the phone line. It was now around midnight and into August 9, 1969.

Backing their car down to the bottom of the hill that led up to the place, they parked it there and walked back up. Thinking the gate might be electrified or rigged with an alarm,[58] they climbed a brushy embankment at its right and dropped onto the grounds. Just then, headlights came their way from farther within the angled property. Telling the girls to lie in the bushes, Watson stepped out with a command to halt and shot to death Steven Parent, eighteen-year-old driver of the approaching car.[56][59] After Watson had prepared their entry to the main house by cutting the screen of an open window, he told Kasabian to keep watch down by the gate.[56][58][54] Entering the house through the slit screen, Watson let Atkins and Krenwinkel in through the front door.[58]

As Watson whispered to Atkins, Roman Polanski's friend Wojciech Frykowski awoke on the living-room couch; Watson kicked him in the head.[56] When Frykowski asked him who he was and what he was doing there, Watson replied, "I'm the devil, and I'm here to do the devil's business."[58][56]

On Watson's direction, Atkins found the house's three other occupants and, with Krenwinkel's help,[58][60] brought them to the living room.

The three were Sharon Tate, eight and a half months pregnant; her friend and former lover Jay Sebring, a noted hairstylist; and Frykowski's lover Abigail Folger, heiress to the Folger coffee fortune.[40] Polanski, Tate's husband, was in London, England, at work on a film project.[61]

As Watson began to tie Tate and Sebring together, by their necks, with rope he'd brought and slung up over a beam, Sebring's protest — his second — of rough treatment of Tate prompted Watson to shoot him. After Folger was taken momentarily back to her bedroom for her purse, which proved to hold about seventy dollars, Watson stabbed the groaning Sebring seven times.[40][56]

Frykowski, whose hands had been bound with a towel, freed himself and began struggling with Atkins, who had been guarding him. As he fought his way toward and out the front door, onto the porch, Watson, who joined in against him, struck him over the head with the gun multiple times (breaking the gun's right grip in the process), stabbed him repeatedly, and shot him twice.[56] Around this time, Kasabian, drawn up from the driveway by "horrifying sounds," arrived outside the door and, in a vain effort to halt the massacre, told Atkins falsely that someone was coming.[54][56]

Inside the house, Folger had escaped from Krenwinkel and fled out a bedroom door to the pool area.[62][63] Pursued to the front lawn by Krenwinkel, who stabbed and, finally, tackled her, she was dispatched by Watson; her two assailants stabbed her a total of twenty-eight times.[56][40] As Frykowski struggled across the lawn, Watson finished him as well, with furious stabbing that brought his total stab wounds to fifty-one.[56][54][40]

Back in the house, Atkins, Watson, or both killed Tate, who was stabbed a total of sixteen times.[40] Tate pleaded to be allowed to live long enough to have her baby; she cried, "Mother... mother..." — until she was dead.[56] (In initial confessions, to cellmates of hers at Sybil Brand Institute, Atkins would say she killed Tate.[64] In later statements — to her attorney, to Vincent Bugliosi, and before a grand jury — she would indicate Tate had been stabbed by Tex Watson.[14][58] In his 1978 autobiography, Watson himself said that he stabbed Tate and that Atkins did not.[56] Aware prosecutor Bugliosi and the jury that had tried the other Tate-LaBianca defendants were convinced Atkins had stabbed Tate, he falsely testified he did not stab her.[65])

Earlier, as the four Family members had headed out from Spahn Ranch, Manson had told the girls to "leave a sign… something witchy."[56] Now, using the towel that had bound Frykowski's hands, Atkins wrote "pig" on the house's front door, in Tate's blood.

En route home, the killers changed out of bloody clothes, which, along with their weapons, they ditched in the hills.[56][64][58]

LaBianca Murders

The next night, six Family members, including the four from night one, rode out at Manson's instruction. Displeased by the panic of the victims at Cielo Drive, Manson accompanied the six, "to show [them] how to do it."[58][54][66] After a few hours' ride, in which he considered a number of murders and even attempted one of them,[54][66] Manson gave Kasabian directions that brought the group to 3301 Waverly Drive, home of supermarket executive Leno LaBianca and his wife, Rosemary, a dress shop co-owner.[59][67] Located in the Los Feliz section of Los Angeles, the LaBianca home was next door to a house at which Manson and Family members had attended a party the previous year.[58][68]

After walking up the driveway and looking in a window, Manson took Watson with him through the unlocked back door.[66] (Atkins and Kasabian would tell prosecutors Manson went up to the house alone, returned with a report that he had tied up the house's occupants, and sent Watson up with Krenwinkel and Van Houten.[58][54] In his autobiography, Watson indicated that, after first going up alone, Manson brought him into the house. He added that, at trial, he "went along with" the others' account, which he figured made him "look that much less responsible.")[65]

Rousing the sleeping Leno LaBianca from the couch at gunpoint, Manson had Watson bind his hands with a leather thong. After Rosemary LaBianca was brought briefly into the living room from the bedroom, Watson followed Manson's instructions to cover the couple's heads with pillowcases, which he bound in place with lamp cord. Manson left, sending Krenwinkel and Leslie Van Houten into the house with instructions that the couple be killed.[66][58][54]

Before leaving Spahn Ranch, Watson had complained to Manson of the inadequacy of the previous night's weapons.[54] Now, sending the girls from the kitchen to the bedroom, to which Rosemary LaBianca had been returned, he went to the living room and began stabbing Leno LaBianca with a chrome-plated bayonet, the first thrust going into the man's throat.

Sounds of a scuffle in the bedroom drew Watson there to discover Mrs. LaBianca keeping the girls at bay by swinging the lamp tied to her neck. Subduing her with several stabs of the bayonet, Watson returned to the living room and resumed attacking Leno, whom he stabbed a total of twelve times. After Watson was done, he carved "WAR" on the man's exposed stomach. (Atkins, who did not enter the LaBianca house, told prosecutors that she believed that Krenwinkel had carved "WAR" on Leno LaBianca's stomach; Watson's autobiography makes clear that he had done it.)[58][66]

Returning to the bedroom, where Krenwinkel was stabbing Rosemary LaBianca with a knife from the LaBianca kitchen, Watson — heeding Manson's instruction to make sure each of the girls played a part — told Van Houten to stab her too.[66] She did, on the exposed buttocks and elsewhere.[68][60][62] (Many of Rosemary LaBianca's forty-one total stab wounds would prove to have been inflicted post-mortem, a fact that would lend support to Leslie Van Houten's equivocal contention that Rosemary LaBianca was dead by the time she stabbed her.)[69]

While Watson cleaned off the bayonet and showered, Krenwinkel wrote "Rise" and "Death to pigs" on the walls and "Healter [sic] Skelter" on the refrigerator door, all in blood. She gave Leno LaBianca fourteen puncture wounds with an ivory-handled, two-tined carving fork, which she left jutting out of his stomach; she also planted a steak knife in his throat.[66][58][54]

Hoping for a double crime, Manson had gone on to direct Kasabian to drive to the Venice home of an actor acquaintance of hers, another "piggy." Depositing the second trio of Family members at the man's apartment building, he drove back to Spahn Ranch, leaving them and the LaBianca killers to hitchhike home.[58][54] Kasabian thwarted this murder by deliberately knocking on the wrong apartment door and waking a stranger. As the group abandoned the murder plan and left, Susan Atkins defecated in the stairwell.[70]

Justice System

Investigation and Arrest

On August 10, 1969 — while the Tate autopsies were under way and the LaBianca bodies were yet to be discovered — detectives of the Los Angeles County Sheriff's Department, which had jurisdiction in the Hinman case, informed LAPD detectives assigned to the Tate case of the bloody writing at the Hinman house. They even mentioned that the Hinman suspect, Beausoleil, was associated with a group of hippies led by "a guy named Charlie." The Tate team, thinking the

Tate murders a consequence of a drug transaction, ignored the information.[40]

Parent, the shooting victim in the Tate driveway, was determined to have been an acquaintance of William Garretson, a young man hired by Rudi Altobelli to take care of the property while Altobelli himself was away.[40] As the killers arrived, Parent had been leaving Cielo Drive, after a visit to Garretson.[40] Held briefly as a Tate suspect, Garretson, who lived in the guest house and told police he had neither seen nor heard anything on the murder night, was released on August 11, 1969.[40][67]

On August 12, 1969, LAPD told the press it had ruled out any connection between the Tate and LaBianca homicides.[67] On August 16, the sheriff's office raided Spahn Ranch and arrested Manson and twenty-five others, as "suspects in a major auto theft ring" that had been stealing Volkswagens and converting them into dune buggies. Weapons were seized, but because the warrant had been misdated the group was released a few days later.[71]

By the end of August, when virtually all leads had gone nowhere, a report by the LaBianca detectives, generally younger than the Tate team, noted a possible connection between the bloody writings at the LaBianca house and "the singing group the Beatles' most recent album."[72]

In mid-October, the LaBianca team, still working separately from the Tate team, checked with the sheriff's office about possible similar crimes and learned of the Hinman case. They also learned that the Hinman detectives had spoken with Beausoleil's girlfriend, Kitty Lutesinger, who had been arrested a few days earlier with members of "the Manson Family."[49]

The arrests had taken place at the desert ranches, to which the Family had moved and where, unknown to authorities, its members had been in the midst of a search for a hole in the ground — access to the Bottomless Pit.[39][73] Known to authorities was that someone had set fire to a piece of earthmoving equipment in the area.[74][75] Raiding the Myers and Barker ranches, authorities had found stolen dune buggies and other vehicles and had arrested two dozen persons, including

Manson. Manson was found hiding in a cabinet beneath a bathroom sink at Barker.[49][74]

A month after they, too, had spoken with Lutesinger, the LaBianca detectives made contact with members of a motorcycle gang she'd told them Manson had tried to enlist as his bodyguards while the Family was at Spahn Ranch.[49] While the gang members were providing information that suggested a link between Manson and the murders,[64][26] a dormitory mate of Susan Atkins succeeded in informing LAPD of the Family's involvement in the crimes.[26] One of those arrested at Barker, Atkins had been booked for the Hinman murder after she'd confirmed to the sheriff's detectives that she'd been involved in it, as Lutesinger had said.[49] Transferred to Sybil Brand Institute, a detention center in Los Angeles, she had begun talking to bunkmates Ronnie Howard and Virginia Graham, whom she gave chilling accounts of the events in which she had been involved.[46]

On December 1, 1969, acting on the information from these sources, LAPD announced warrants for the arrest of Watson, Krenwinkel, and Kasabian in the Tate case; the suspects' involvement in the LaBianca murders was noted. Manson and Atkins, already in custody, were not mentioned; the connection between the LaBianca case and Van Houten, who was also among those arrested near Death Valley, had not yet been recognized.[74][20][58]

Watson and Krenwinkel, too, were already under arrest, authorities in Texas and Alabama having picked them up on notice from LAPD.[20] On December 2, in New Hampshire, Kasabian voluntarily surrendered to authorities.[20]

Conviction and Sentencing

At the trial, which began June 15, 1970,[60] the prosecution's main witness was Kasabian, who, along with Manson, Atkins, and Krenwinkel, had been charged with seven counts of murder and one of conspiracy.[21] Not having participated in the killings, she was granted immunity in exchange for testimony that detailed the nights of crimes.[22][17][76] On Friday, July 24, the first day of testimony, Manson appeared in court with an X carved into his forehead; he issued a statement that he had "X'd [him]self from [the establishment's] world."[77] Duplicated over the following weekend by the female defendants and, within another day or two, by most Family members, the mark was graphic evidence of Manson's domination.[78]

The prosecution placed the triggering of Helter Skelter as the main motive.[79] The crime scenes' bloody White Album references — pig, rise, helter skelter — were correlated with testimony about Manson predictions that the murders blacks would commit at the outset of Helter Skelter would involve the writing of "pigs" on walls in victims' blood.[36][80] Testimony that Manson had said "now is the time for Helter Skelter" was supplemented with Kasabian's testimony that, on the night of the LaBianca murders, Manson considered discarding Rosemary LaBianca's wallet on the street of a black neighborhood.[54] Having obtained the wallet in the LaBianca house, he "wanted a black person to pick it up and use the credit cards so that the people, the establishment, would think it was some sort of an organized group that killed these people."[81] On his direction, Kasabian had hidden it in the women's rest room of a service station near a black area.[58][82][54][42] "I want to show blackie how to do it," Manson had said as the Family members had driven along after the departure from the LaBianca house.[81]

During the trial, Family members haunted the entrances and corridors of the courthouse and were denied access to the courtroom itself only by being subpoenaed as prospective prosecution witnesses.[83] When the group established itself in vigil on the sidewalk, each hard-core member wore a sheathed hunting knife that, being in plain view, was being carried legally. Each was identifiable by the X on his or her forehead.[84]

On August 4, despite precautions taken by the court, Manson flashed the jury a Los Angeles Times front page whose headline was "Manson Guilty, Nixon Declares," a reference to a statement made the previous day when U.S. President Richard Nixon had decried what he saw as the media's glamorization of Manson. Voir dired by Judge Charles Older, the jurors contended that the headline had not influenced them. The next day, the female defendants stood up and said in unison that, in light of the President's remark, there was no point in going on with the trial.[85] On October 5, denied the court's permission to question a prosecution witness whom the defense attorneys had declined to cross-examine, Manson leaped over the defense table and attempted to attack Judge Charles Older. Wrestled to the ground by bailiffs, he was removed from the courtroom with the female defendants, who'd subsequently risen and begun chanting in Latin.[42] Thereafter, Older allegedly began wearing a revolver under his robes.[42]

As the body of the trial concluded and with the closing arguments impending, attorney Ronald Hughes, who had been representing Leslie Van Houten, disappeared during a weekend trip.[86] When Maxwell Keith was appointed to represent Van Houten in Hughes's absence, a delay of more than two weeks was required to permit Keith to familiarize himself with the voluminous trial transcripts.[86] No sooner had the trial resumed, just before Christmas, than disruptions of the prosecution's closing argument by the defendants led Older to ban the four from the courtroom for the remainder of the guilt phase. Older said that, after "lo, these many months," it was obvious that the defendants were "operating in concert with each other" and using the court "as a stage for some kind of performance."[87]

On January 25, 1971, guilty verdicts were returned against Manson, Krenwinkel and Atkins on the seven counts of murder and the one of conspiracy; Van Houten was convicted on two counts of murder and one of conspiracy.[88] In the trial's guilt phase, the defendants had shocked the court by resting without calling a single witness. Lawyers for the women had been unwilling to let Manson engineer a defense in which their clients would testify and take all guilt upon themselves.[89] Not far into the penalty phase, the jurors got a glimpse of the defense Manson had had in mind. Atkins, Krenwinkel, and Van Houten testified the murders had been conceived as "copycat" versions of the Hinman murder, for which Atkins now took credit. The killings, they said, were intended to draw suspicion away from Bobby Beausoleil, by resembling the crime for which he had been jailed. This plan had supposedly been the work of, and carried out under the guidance of, not Manson, but someone allegedly in love with Beausoleil — Linda Kasabian.[90] Among the narrative's weak points was Atkins's inability to explain why, as she was maintaining, she had written "political piggy" at the Hinman house in the first place.[90][80]

Midway through the penalty phase, Manson shaved his head and trimmed his beard to a fork; he told the press, "I am the Devil, and the Devil always has a bald head."[91] In what the prosecution regarded as belated recognition on their part that imitation of Manson only proved his domination, the female defendants refrained from shaving their heads until the jurors retired to weigh the state's request for the death penalty.[91][92]

The effort to exonerate Manson via the "copycat" scenario failed; on 29 March 1971, the jury returned verdicts of death against all four defendants on all counts.[80] On 19 April 1971, Judge Older sentenced the four to death.[93]

On the day the verdicts recommending the death penalty were returned, news came that the badly-decomposed body of Ronald Hughes had been found wedged between two boulders in Ventura County.[94] It was rumored, although never proven, that Hughes was murdered by the Family, possibly because he had stood up to Manson and refused to allow Leslie Van Houten to take the stand and absolve Manson of the crimes.[95] A Family member allegedly said Hughes was "the first of the retaliation murders." [96]

Aftermath

Protracted proceedings to extradite Tex Watson from his native Texas,[68][63][97] where he had resettled a month before his arrest,[98] resulted in his being tried separately. The trial commenced in August 1971; by October, he, too, had been found guilty on seven counts of murder and one of conspiracy. He, too, was sentenced to death.[57]

In February 1972, the death sentences of all five parties were automatically reduced to life in prison by California v. Anderson 64 Cal.2d 633, 414 P.2d 366, (Cal. 1972), in which the Supreme Court of California abolished the death penalty in that state.[99]

In a 1971 trial that took place after his Tate-LaBianca convictions, Manson was found guilty of the murders of Gary Hinman and Donald "Shorty" Shea and was given a life sentence. Shea, a Spahn Ranch stuntman and horse wrangler, had been killed approximately ten days after the 16 August 1969, sheriff's raid on the ranch. Manson, who suspected that Shea helped set up the raid, had apparently believed Shea was trying to get George Spahn to run the Family off the ranch. Manson was annoyed, too, that the white Shea had married a black woman; and it's possible Shea knew about the Tate-LaBianca killings.[26][100] In separate trials, Family members Bruce Davis and Steve "Clem" Grogan were also found guilty of Shea's murder.[26][57][101]

Before the conclusion of Manson's Tate-LaBianca trial, a reporter for the Los Angeles Times tracked down Manson's mother, remarried and living in the Pacific Northwest. The former Kathleen Maddox indicated that, in childhood, her son had known no neglect; he had even been "pampered by all the women who surrounded him."[8]

On September 5, 1975, Squeaky Fromme attempted to assassinate U.S. President Gerald Ford in Sacramento, to which she and Manson follower Sandra Good had moved to be near Manson while he was incarcerated at Folsom State Prison. A subsequent search of the apartment shared by Fromme, Good, and a Family recruit turned up evidence that, coupled with later actions on the part of Good, resulted in Good's conviction for conspiring to send threatening communications through the United States mail and transmitting death threats by way of interstate commerce. (The threats that were involved were against corporate executives and US government officials and had to do with supposed environmental dereliction on their part.)[102]

1977 marked the resolution of a longstanding Family mystery — the precise location of the remains of Shorty Shea and whether, as had been claimed, Shea had been dismembered and buried in several places. Contacting the prosecutor in his case, Steve Grogan told him that Shea's corpse had been buried in one piece; he drew a map that pinpointed the location of the body, which was recovered. Of those convicted of Manson-ordered murders, Grogan would become, in 1985, the first to be paroled — and, as of 2007, the only one.[103]

In the 1980s, Manson gave three notable interviews. The first, recorded at California Medical Facility and aired June 13, 1981, was by Tom Snyder for NBC's The Tomorrow Show. The second, recorded at San Quentin Prison and aired March 7, 1986, was by Charlie Rose for CBS News Nightwatch; it won the national news Emmy Award for "Best Interview" in 1987.[104] The last, with Geraldo Rivera in 1988, was part of that journalist's prime-time special on Satanism.[105]

In December 1987, Fromme, serving a life sentence for the assassination attempt, escaped briefly from Alderson Federal Prison Camp in West Virginia. She was trying to reach Manson, whom she had heard had cancer; she was apprehended within days.[102]

In a 1994 conversation with Manson prosecutor Vincent Bugliosi, one-time Manson-follower Catherine Share stated that her testimony in the penalty phase of Manson's trial had been a fabrication intended to save Manson from the gas chamber and had been given on Manson's explicit direction.[102] Share's testimony had introduced the copycat-motive story, which the testimony of the three female defendants echoed and according to which the Tate-LaBianca murders had been the idea of Linda Kasabian.[90] In a 1997 segment of the tabloid television program Hard Copy, Share implied that her testimony had been given under a Manson threat of physical harm.[106] In August 1971, after Manson's trial and sentencing, Share had participated in a violent California retail-store robbery, the object of which was the acquisition of weapons to help free Manson.[57]

In January 1996, a Manson web site was established by latter-day Manson follower George Stimson, who was helped by Sandra Good. Good had been released from prison in 1985, after serving ten years of her fifteen-year sentence for the death threats.[102][107]

In a 1998-9 interview in Seconds magazine, Bobby Beausoleil rejected the view that Manson ordered him to kill Gary Hinman.[52] He stated

Manson did come to Hinman's house and slash Hinman with a sword. In a 1981 interview with Oui magazine, he denied this. Beausoleil stated that when he read about the Tate murders in the newspaper, "I wasn't even sure at that point — really, I had no idea who had done it until Manson's group were actually arrested for it. It had only crossed my mind and I had a premonition, perhaps. There was some little tickle in my mind that the killings might be connected with them...." In the Oui magazine interview, he had stated, "When [the Tate-LaBianca murders] happened, I knew who had done it. I was fairly certain."[51]

William Garretson, once the young caretaker at Cielo Drive, indicated in a program broadcast in July 1999 on E!, that he had, in fact, seen and heard a portion of the Tate murders from his location in the property's guest house. This comported with the unofficial results of a polygraph examination that had been given to Garretson on August 10, 1969, and that had effectively eliminated him as a suspect.[108] The LAPD officer who conducted the examination had concluded Garretson was "clean" on participation in the crimes but "muddy" as to his having heard anything.[40] Garretson did not explain why he had withheld his knowledge of the events.[109]

On 5 September 2007, MSNBC aired The Mind of Manson, a complete version of a 1987 interview at California's San Quentin State Prison. The footage of the "unshackled, unapologetic, and unruly" Manson had been considered "so unbelievable" that only seven minutes of it had originally been broadcast on The Today Show, for which it had been recorded.[110]

Parole Hearings

On 23 May 2007, Manson was denied parole for the eleventh time.[111] He will not be eligible again for parole until 2012. He is an inmate in the Protective Housing Unit at Corcoran State Prison in Corcoran, California.[112] His inmate number in the California Department of Corrections and Rehabilitation is B33920.

Manson and Culture

Recordings

March 6, 1970, the day the court vacated Manson's status as his own attorney,[54] saw the release of LIE, an album of Manson music.[113][114] This included "Cease to Exist," a Manson composition the Beach Boys had recorded with modified lyrics and the title "Never Learn Not to Love."[115][116] Over the next couple of months, only about three hundred of the album's two thousand copies sold.[117]

Since that time, there have been several releases of Manson recordings — music and speech.[118] The Family Jams includes two compact discs of Manson's songs recorded by the Family in 1970, after Manson and the others had been arrested. Guitar and lead vocals are supplied by Steve Grogan;[74] additional vocals are supplied by Lynette Fromme, Sandra Good, Catherine Share, and others.[118][119]

American rock band Guns N' Roses drew heavy criticism for recording Manson's "Look at Your Game, Girl," included as an unlisted thirteenth track on their 1993 album "The Spaghetti Incident?"[99][120][121] "My Monkey," which appears on the first album by Marilyn Manson (no relation, as is explained below), includes the lyrics "I had a little monkey/I sent him to the country and I fed him on gingerbread/Along came a choo-choo/Knocked my monkey cuckoo/And now my monkey's dead."[122] These are from Charles Manson's "Mechancial Man,"[123] which is heard on LIE.

Cultural Reverberation

Within months of the Tate-LaBianca arrests, Manson was embraced by underground newspapers of the 1960s counterculture from which the Family had emerged.[117][124] When a Rolling Stone writer visited the Los Angeles District Attorney's office for a June 1970 cover story,[125] he was shocked by a photograph of the bloody "Healter [sic] Skelter" that would bind Manson to popular culture.[126]

Manson's influence has ranged wide, in pop culture and beyond, covering fashion,[127][128] graphics,[129][130] music,[131] movies, television, and the stage. In an afterword composed for the 1994 edition of the non-fiction Helter Skelter, prosecutor Vincent Bugliosi quoted a BBC employee's assertion that a "neo-Manson cult" existing then in Europe was represented by, among other things, approximately seventy rock bands playing songs by Manson and "songs in support of him."[99]

Just one specimen of popular music with Manson references is Alkaline Trio's "Sadie," whose lyrics include the phrases "Sadie G," "Ms. Susan A," and "Charlie's broken .22."[132] "Sadie Mae Glutz" was the name by which Susan Atkins was known within the Family,[49][50] and the pistol whose grip shattered when Tex Watson used it to bludgeon Wojciech Frykowski was a twenty-two caliber.[56] "Sadie's" lyrics are followed by a spoken passage derived from Atkins's testimony in the penalty phase of the trial of Manson and the women.[133][134]

Manson has even influenced the names of musical performers such as Spahn Ranch and Marilyn Manson, the latter a stage name assembled from "Charles Manson" and "Marilyn Monroe."[135] The story of the Family's activities inspired John Moran's opera The Manson Family and Stephen Sondheim's musical Assassins, the latter of which has Lynette Fromme as a character.[136][137] The tale has been the subject of several movies, including two television dramatizations of Helter Skelter.[138][139] In the South Park episode Merry Christmas Charlie Manson, Manson is a comic character whose inmate number is 06660, an apparent reference to 666, the Biblical "number of the beast."[140][141]

Helter Skelter and Beyond

Documentaries

* Manson, directed by Robert Hendrickson and Laurence Merrick. 1973. Entry at imdb.com
* Charles Manson Superstar, directed by Nikolas Schreck. 1989. Entry at imdb.com

Helter Skelter and Beyond

References

1. Linder, Doug. The Charles Manson (Tate-LaBianca Murder) Trial. UMKC Law. 2002. Retrieved 7 April 2007.

2. Bugliosi, Vincent with Gentry, Curt. Helter Skelter — The True Story of the Manson Murders 25th Anniversary Edition, W.W. Norton & Company, 1994. ISBN 0-393-08700-X. Pages 163-4, 313.

3. Smith, David E. and Rose, Alan J. A Case Study of the Charles Manson Group Marriage Commune. Journal of the American Society of Psychosomatic Dentistry and Medicine, 1970. 17(3):99-106.

4. Prosecution's closing argument. Page 1 of multi-page transcript, 2violent.com. Retrieved 16 April 2007.

5. History of California's Death Penalty deathpenalty.org. Retrieved 5 December 2007.

6.   Bugliosi 1994, p. 136-7.

7.   Emmons, Nuel. Manson in His Own Words. Grove Press, New York; 1988. ISBN 0-8021-3024-0.

8.   Smith, Dave. Mother Tells Life of Manson as Boy. 1971 article copy on Manson Family Today.info. Retrieved June 5, 2007.

9.   Reitwiesner, William Addams. Provisional ancestry of Charles Manson. Retrieved 26 April 2007.

10.   Photocopy of Manson birth certifcate MansonDirect.com. Retrieved 26 April 2007.

11.   Bugliosi, p. 137-146.

12.   1981 Tom Snyder interview with Charles Manson. Transcribed by Aaron Bredlau. CharlieManson.com. Retrieved 26 April 2007.

13.   Karpis, Alvin, with Robert Livesey. On the Rock: Twenty-five Years at Alcatraz, 1980.

14. Bugliosi, 1994. pp. 163-174.

15. Bugliosi 1994, 144, 163-64.

16. Sanders, Ed. The Family, Thunder's Mouth Press, New York, 2002. ISBN 1-56025-396-7. Pages 13-20.

17. Bugliosi 1994. pp. 250-253.

18. Sanders 2002, p. 34.

19. Watkins, Paul with Soledad, Guillermo. My Life with Charles Manson, Bantam, 1979. ISBN 0-553-12788-8. Chapter 4.

20. Bugliosi 1994. 155-161.

21. Bugliosi 1994. 185-188.

22. Bugliosi 1994. 214-219.

23. Watson, Charles as told to Ray Hoekstra. Will You Die for Me?, Chapter 9 Watson website. Retrieved May 3, 2007.

24. Watson, Ch. 6.

25. Watson, Ch. 7.

26. Bugliosi 1994. pp. 99-113.

27. Watkins, pages 34 & 40.

28. Watson, Ch. 4.

29. Watkins, Ch. 10.

30. Watkins, Ch. 11.

31. Chapter 1, "Manson," Manson's Right-Hand Man Speaks Out!. ISBN 0-9678519-1-2. Retrieved November 21, 2007.

32. Watkins, Ch. 12.

33. Sanders 2002, 11.

34. Watson, Ch. 11.

35. The Influence of the Beatles on Charles Manson. UMKC Law. Retrieved 7 April 2006.

36. Bugliosi 1994, 244-247.

37. Watkins, p. 137.

38. Testimony of Paul Watkins in the Charles Manson Trial UMKC Law. Retrieved 7 April 2007.

39. Bugliosi 1994, 228-233.

40. Bugliosi 1994, 28-38.

41. Bugliosi 1994, 226.

42. Bugliosi 1994, 369-377.

43. Watson, Ch. 12.

44. Watkins, Ch. 15.

45. Watson, Ch. 13.

46. Bugliosi 1994, 91-96.

47. Sanders 2002, 147-49.

48. Sanders 2002, 151.

49. Bugliosi 1994, 75-77.

50. Atkins, Susan, with Bob Slosser. Child of Satan, Child of God; Logos International, Plainfield, New Jersey; 1977; ISBN 0-88270-276-9; pages 94-120.

51. Beausoleil Oui interview. Charlie Manson.com.

52. Beausoleil Seconds interviews. Charlie Manson.com.

53. Sanders 2002, page 184.

54. Bugliosi 1994, 258-269.

55. Prosecution's closing argument Page 6 of multi-page transcript, 2violent.com.

56. Watson, Ch. 14.

57. Bugliosi 1994, 463-468.

58. Bugliosi 1994, 176-184.

59. Bugliosi 1994, 22-25.

60. Bugliosi 1994, 297-300.

61. Bugliosi 1994, 10-14.

62. Bugliosi 1994, 341-344.

63. Bugliosi 1994, 356-361.

64. Bugliosi 1994, 84-90.

65. Watson, Ch. 19.

66. Watson, Ch. 15.

67. Bugliosi 1994, 42-48.

68. Bugliosi 1994, 204-210.

69. Bugliosi 1994; pp. 44, 206, 297, 341-42, 380, 404, 406-07, 433.

70. Bugliosi 1994, 270-273.

71. Bugliosi 1994, 56.

72. Bugliosi 1994, 65.

73. Watkins, Ch. 21.

74. Bugliosi 1994, 125-127.

75. Watkins, Ch. 22

76. Bugliosi 1994, 330-332.

77. Bugliosi 1994, 310.

78. Bugliosi 1994, 316.

79. Prosecution's closing argument Page 29 of multi-page transcript, 2violent.com.

80. Bugliosi 1994, 450-457.

81. Prosecution's closing argument Pages 22-23 of multi-page transcript, 2violent.com.

82. Bugliosi 1994, 190-91.

83. Bugliosi 1994, 309.

84. Bugliosi 1994, 339.

85. Bugliosi 1994, 323-328.

86. Bugliosi 1994, 393-398.

87. Bugliosi 1994, 399-407.

88. Bugliosi 1994, 411-419.

89. Bugliosi 1994, 380-89.

90. Bugliosi 1994, 424-433.

91. Bugliosi 1994, 439.

92. Bugliosi 1994, 455.

93. Bugliosi 1994, 458-459.

94. Bugliosi 1994, 457.

95. Bugliosi 1994, 387, 394, 481.

96. Bugliosi 1994, 481-82.

97. Watson, Ch. 18.

98. Watson, Ch. 16.

99. Bugliosi 1994, 488-491.

100. Sanders 2002, 271-2.

101. Transcript of Charles Manson's 1992 parole hearing University of Missouri-Kansas City School of Law. Retrieved May 24, 2007.

102. Bugliosi 1994, 502-511.

103. Bugliosi 1994, 509.

104. Joynt, Carol. Diary of a Mad Saloon Owner. April-May 2005.

105. Rivera's 'Devil Worship' was TV at Its Worst Review by Tom Shales. Transcribed from

San Jose Mercury News, 31 October 1988. Retrieved 28 November 2007.

106.   Catherine Share with Vincent Bugliosi, Hard Copy, 1997 youtube.com. Retrieved May 30, 2007.

107.   Manson's Family Affair Living in Cyberspace. wired.com, 16 April 1997. Retrieved May 29, 2007.

108.   Transcript of William Garretson polygraph exam. CharlieManson.com. Retrieved June 10, 2007.

109.   Transcript and synopsis of William Garretson comments. "The Last Days of Sharon Tate," The E! True Hollywood Story. CharlieManson.com. Retrieved June 10, 2007.

110.   Transcript, MSNBC Live. 5 September 2007. Retrieved November 21, 2007.

111.   72-year-old Charles Manson denied parole. Reuters, 24 May 2007. Daily Telegraph (Australia). Retrieved September 6, 2007.

112. Life Prisoner Parole Consideration Hearings May 7, 2007 - June 2, 2007. Board of Parole Hearings, Calif. Dept. of Corrections and Rehabilitation. P. 3. Retrieved May 2, 2007.

113. Sanders 2002, 336.

114. Lie: The Love And Terror Cult. ASIN: B000005X1J. Amazon.com. Access date: 23 November 2007.

115. Sanders 2002, 64-65.

116. Dennis Wilson interview Circus magazine, October 26, 1976. Retrieved 1 December 2007.

117. Rolling Stone story on Manson, June 1970 CharlieManson.com. Retrieved May 2, 2007.

118. List of Manson recordings mansondirect.com. Retrieved November 24, 2007.

119. The Family Jams. ASIN: B0002UXM2Q. 2004. Amazon.com.

120. Review of The Spaghetti Incident? allmusic.com. Retrieved November 23, 2007.

121. Guns N' Roses biography rollingstone.com. Retrieved November 23, 2007.

122. Lyrics of "My Monkey" sing365.com. Retrieved January 22, 2008.

123. Lyrics of "Mechanical Man" charliemanson.com. Retrieved January 22, 2008.

124. Bugliosi 1994, 221-22.

125. Manson on cover of Rolling Stone rollingstone.com. Retrieved May 2, 2007.

126. Dalton, David. If Christ Came Back as a Con Man. gadflyonline.com. Retrieved 30 September 2007.

127. Bant Shirts Manson T-shirt.

128. Prank Place Manson T-shirt.
129. "No Name Maddox" Manson portrait in marijuana seeds. Retrieved November 23, 2007.

130. Poster of Manson on cover of Rolling Stone.

131. The Metal Observer Review of Generator, 2006 album by Aborym. Retrieved 26 April 2007.

132. Lyrics of "Sadie," by Alkaline Trio sing365.com. Retrieved November 23, 2007.

133. Bugliosi 1994, 428-29.

134. Alkaline Trio on MySpace Includes full-length audio of "Sadie." Retrieved 2 December 2007.

135. Biography for Marilyn Manson imdb.com. Retrieved 23 November 2007.

136. Will the Manson Story Play as Myth, Operatically at That? New York Times, 17 July 1990. Retrieved 23 November 2007.

137. Sondheim.com Assassins.

138. Helter Skelter (2004) imdb.com.

139. Helter Skelter (1976) imdb.com.

140. Merry Christmas Charlie Manson Video clips at southpark.comedycentral.com.

141. Beast Number WolframMathWorld. Retrieved 29 November 2007.

Primary

* Atkins, Susan with Bob Slosser. Child of Satan, Child of God. Logos International; Plainfield, New Jersey; 1977. ISBN 0-88270-276-9.

* Bugliosi, Vincent with Curt Gentry. Helter Skelter: The True Story of the Manson Murders. (Norton, 1974; Arrow books, 1992 edition, ISBN 0-09-997500-9; W. W. Norton & Company, 2001, ISBN 0-393-32223-8).

* Emmons, Nuel, as told to. Manson in His Own Words. Grove Press, 1988. ISBN 0-8021-3024-0.

* Sanders, Ed The Family. Thunder's Mouth Press. rev. update edition 2002. ISBN 1-56025-396-7.

* Watkins, Paul with Guillermo Soledad. My Life with Charles Manson. Bantam, 1979. ISBN 0-553-12788-8.

* Watson, Charles. Will you die for me?. F. H. Revell, 1978. ISBN 0-8007-0912-8.

Further Reading

* George, Edward and Dary Matera. Taming the Beast: Charles Manson's Life Behind Bars. St. Martin's Press, 1999. ISBN 0-312-20970-3.

* Gilmore, John. Manson: The Unholy Trail of Charlie and the Family. Amok Books, 2000. ISBN 1-878923-13-7.

* Gilmore, John. The Garbage People. Omega Press, 1971.

* LeBlanc, Jerry and Ivor Davis. 5 to Die. Holloway House Publishing, 1971. ISBN 0-87067-306-8.

* Pellowski, Michael J. The Charles Manson Murder Trial: A Headline Court Case. Enslow Publishers, 2004. ISBN 0-7660-2167-X.

* Rowlett, Curt. Labyrinth13: True Tales of the Occult, Crime & Conspiracy, Chapter 10, Charles Manson, Son of Sam and the Process Church of the Final Judgment: Exploring the Alleged

Connections. Lulu Press, 2006. ISBN 1-4116-6083-8.

* Schreck, Nikolas. The Manson File Amok Press. 1988. ISBN 0-941693-04-X.

* Udo, Tommy. Charles Manson: Music, Mayhem, Murder. Sanctuary Records, 2002. ISBN 1-86074-388-9.

Charles Manson

GNU Free Documentation License

Version 1.2, November 2002

0. PREAMBLE

The purpose of this License is to make a manual, textbook, or other
functional and useful document "free" in the sense of freedom: to assure
everyone the effective freedom to copy and redistribute it, with or without
modifying it, either commercially or noncommercially. Secondarily, this
License preserves for the author and publisher a way to get credit for their
work, while not being considered responsible for modifications made by
others.

This License is a kind of "copyleft", which means that derivative works of
the document must themselves be free in the same sense. It complements
the GNU General Public License, which is a copyleft license designed for
free software.

We have designed this License in order to use it for manuals for free
software, because free software needs free documentation: a free program
should come with manuals providing the same freedoms that the software
does. But this License is not limited to software manuals; it can be used for
any textual work, regardless of subject matter or whether it is published as a
printed book. We recommend this License principally for works whose
purpose is instruction or reference.

Helter Skelter and Beyond

1. APPLICABILITY AND DEFINITIONS

This License applies to any manual or other work, in any medium, that contains a notice placed by the copyright holder saying it can be distributed under the terms of this License. Such a notice grants a world-wide, royalty-free license, unlimited in duration, to use that work under the conditions stated herein. The "Document", below, refers to any such manual or work. Any member of the public is a licensee, and is addressed as "you". You accept the license if you copy, modify or distribute the work in a way requiring permission under copyright law.

A "Modified Version" of the Document means any work containing the Document or a portion of it, either copied verbatim, or with modifications and/or translated into another language.

A "Secondary Section" is a named appendix or a front-matter section of the Document that deals exclusively with the relationship of the publishers or authors of the Document to the Document's overall subject (or to related matters) and contains nothing that could fall directly within that overall subject. (Thus, if the Document is in part a textbook of mathematics, a Secondary Section may not explain any mathematics.) The relationship could be a matter of historical connection with the subject or with related matters, or of legal, commercial, philosophical, ethical or political position regarding them.

The "Invariant Sections" are certain Secondary Sections whose titles are designated, as being those of Invariant Sections, in the notice that says that the Document is released under this License. If a section does not fit the above definition of Secondary then it is not allowed to be designated as Invariant. The Document may contain zero Invariant Sections. If the Document does not identify any Invariant Sections then there are none.

The "Cover Texts" are certain short passages of text that are listed, as Front-Cover Texts or Back-Cover Texts, in the notice that says that the Document is released under this License. A Front-Cover Text may be at most 5 words, and a Back-Cover Text may be at most 25 words.

Charles Manson

A "Transparent" copy of the Document means a machine-readable copy, represented in a format whose specification is available to the general public, that is suitable for revising the document straightforwardly with generic text editors or (for images composed of pixels) generic paint programs or (for drawings) some widely available drawing editor, and that is suitable for input to text formatters or for automatic translation to a variety of formats suitable for input to text formatters. A copy made in an otherwise Transparent file format whose markup, or absence of markup, has been arranged to thwart or discourage subsequent modification by readers is not Transparent. An image format is not Transparent if used for any substantial amount of text. A copy that is not "Transparent" is called "Opaque".

Examples of suitable formats for Transparent copies include plain ASCII without markup, Texinfo input format, LaTeX input format, SGML or XML using a publicly available DTD, and standard-conforming simple HTML, PostScript or PDF designed for human modification. Examples of transparent image formats include PNG, XCF and JPG. Opaque formats include proprietary formats that can be read and edited only by proprietary word processors, SGML or XML for which the DTD and/or processing tools are not generally available, and the machine-generated HTML, PostScript or PDF produced by some word processors for output purposes only.

The "Title Page" means, for a printed book, the title page itself, plus such following pages as are needed to hold, legibly, the material this License requires to appear in the title page. For works in formats which do not have any title page as such, "Title Page" means the text near the most prominent appearance of the work's title, preceding the beginning of the body of the text.

A section "Entitled XYZ" means a named subunit of the Document whose title either is precisely XYZ or contains XYZ in parentheses following text that translates XYZ in another language. (Here XYZ stands for a specific section name mentioned below, such as "Acknowledgements", "Dedications", "Endorsements", or "History".) To "Preserve the Title" of such a section when you modify the Document means that it remains a section "Entitled XYZ" according to this definition.

Helter Skelter and Beyond

The Document may include Warranty Disclaimers next to the notice which states that this License applies to the Document. These Warranty Disclaimers are considered to be included by reference in this License, but only as regards disclaiming warranties: any other implication that these Warranty Disclaimers may have is void and has no effect on the meaning of this License.

2. VERBATIM COPYING

You may copy and distribute the Document in any medium, either commercially or noncommercially, provided that this License, the copyright notices, and the license notice saying this License applies to the Document are reproduced in all copies, and that you add no other conditions whatsoever to those of this License. You may not use technical measures to obstruct or control the reading or further copying of the copies you make or distribute. However, you may accept compensation in exchange for copies. If you distribute a large enough number of copies you must also follow the conditions in section 3.

You may also lend copies, under the same conditions stated above, and you may publicly display copies.

3. COPYING IN QUANTITY

If you publish printed copies (or copies in media that commonly have printed covers) of the Document, numbering more than 100, and the Document's license notice requires Cover Texts, you must enclose the copies in covers that carry, clearly and legibly, all these Cover Texts: Front-Cover Texts on the front cover, and Back-Cover Texts on the back cover. Both covers must also clearly and legibly identify you as the publisher of these copies. The front cover must present the full title with all words of the title equally prominent and visible. You may add other material on the covers in addition. Copying with changes limited to the covers, as long as they preserve the title of the Document and satisfy these conditions, can be treated as verbatim copying in other respects.

If the required texts for either cover are too voluminous to fit legibly, you should put the first ones listed (as many as fit reasonably) on the actual cover, and continue the rest onto adjacent pages.

Charles Manson

If you publish or distribute Opaque copies of the Document numbering more than 100, you must either include a machine-readable Transparent copy along with each Opaque copy, or state in or with each Opaque copy a computer-network location from which the general network-using public has access to download using public-standard network protocols a complete Transparent copy of the Document, free of added material. If you use the latter option, you must take reasonably prudent steps, when you begin distribution of Opaque copies in quantity, to ensure that this Transparent copy will remain thus accessible at the stated location until at least one year after the last time you distribute an Opaque copy (directly or through your agents or retailers) of that edition to the public.

It is requested, but not required, that you contact the authors of the Document well before redistributing any large number of copies, to give them a chance to provide you with an updated version of the Document.

4. MODIFICATIONS

You may copy and distribute a Modified Version of the Document under the conditions of sections 2 and 3 above, provided that you release the Modified Version under precisely this License, with the Modified Version filling the role of the Document, thus licensing distribution and modification of the Modified Version to whoever possesses a copy of it. In addition, you must do these things in the Modified Version:

   * A. Use in the Title Page (and on the covers, if any) a title distinct from that of the Document, and from those of previous versions (which should, if there were any, be listed in the History section of the Document). You may use the same title as a previous version if the original publisher of that version gives permission.
   * B. List on the Title Page, as authors, one or more persons or entities responsible for authorship of the modifications in the Modified Version, together with at least five of the principal authors of the Document (all of its principal authors, if it has fewer than five), unless they release you from this requirement.
   * C. State on the Title page the name of the publisher of the Modified Version, as the publisher.
   * D. Preserve all the copyright notices of the Document.

* E. Add an appropriate copyright notice for your modifications adjacent to the other copyright notices.

* F. Include, immediately after the copyright notices, a license notice giving the public permission to use the Modified Version under the terms of this License, in the form shown in the Addendum below.

* G. Preserve in that license notice the full lists of Invariant Sections and required Cover Texts given in the Document's license notice.

* H. Include an unaltered copy of this License.

* I. Preserve the section Entitled "History", Preserve its Title, and add to it an item stating at least the title, year, new authors, and publisher of the Modified Version as given on the Title Page. If there is no section Entitled "History" in the Document, create one stating the title, year, authors, and publisher of the Document as given on its Title Page, then add an item describing the Modified Version as stated in the previous sentence.

* J. Preserve the network location, if any, given in the Document for public access to a Transparent copy of the Document, and likewise the network locations given in the Document for previous versions it was based on. These may be placed in the "History" section. You may omit a network location for a work that was published at least four years before the Document itself, or if the original publisher of the version it refers to gives permission.

* K. For any section Entitled "Acknowledgements" or "Dedications", Preserve the Title of the section, and preserve in the section all the substance and tone of each of the contributor acknowledgements and/or dedications given therein.

* L. Preserve all the Invariant Sections of the Document, unaltered in their text and in their titles. Section numbers or the equivalent are not considered part of the section titles.

* M. Delete any section Entitled "Endorsements". Such a section may not be included in the Modified Version.

* N. Do not retitle any existing section to be Entitled "Endorsements" or to conflict in title with any Invariant Section.

* O. Preserve any Warranty Disclaimers.

If the Modified Version includes new front-matter sections or appendices that qualify as Secondary Sections and contain no material copied from the Document, you may at your option designate some or all of these sections as invariant. To do this, add their titles to the list of Invariant Sections in the

Modified Version's license notice. These titles must be distinct from any other section titles.

You may add a section Entitled "Endorsements", provided it contains nothing but endorsements of your Modified Version by various parties--for example, statements of peer review or that the text has been approved by an organization as the authoritative definition of a standard.

You may add a passage of up to five words as a Front-Cover Text, and a passage of up to 25 words as a Back-Cover Text, to the end of the list of Cover Texts in the Modified Version. Only one passage of Front-Cover Text and one of Back-Cover Text may be added by (or through arrangements made by) any one entity. If the Document already includes a cover text for the same cover, previously added by you or by arrangement made by the same entity you are acting on behalf of, you may not add another; but you may replace the old one, on explicit permission from the previous publisher that added the old one.

The author(s) and publisher(s) of the Document do not by this License give permission to use their names for publicity for or to assert or imply endorsement of any Modified Version.

5. COMBINING DOCUMENTS

You may combine the Document with other documents released under this License, under the terms defined in section 4 above for modified versions, provided that you include in the combination all of the Invariant Sections of all of the original documents, unmodified, and list them all as Invariant Sections of your combined work in its license notice, and that you preserve all their Warranty Disclaimers.

The combined work need only contain one copy of this License, and multiple identical Invariant Sections may be replaced with a single copy. If there are multiple Invariant Sections with the same name but different contents, make the title of each such section unique by adding at the end of it, in parentheses, the name of the original author or publisher of that section if known, or else a unique number. Make the same adjustment to the section titles in the list of Invariant Sections in the license notice of the combined work.

In the combination, you must combine any sections Entitled "History" in the various original documents, forming one section Entitled "History"; likewise combine any sections Entitled "Acknowledgements", and any sections Entitled "Dedications". You must delete all sections Entitled "Endorsements."

6. COLLECTIONS OF DOCUMENTS

You may make a collection consisting of the Document and other documents released under this License, and replace the individual copies of this License in the various documents with a single copy that is included in the collection, provided that you follow the rules of this License for verbatim copying of each of the documents in all other respects.

You may extract a single document from such a collection, and distribute it individually under this License, provided you insert a copy of this License into the extracted document, and follow this License in all other respects regarding verbatim copying of that document.

7. AGGREGATION WITH INDEPENDENT WORKS

A compilation of the Document or its derivatives with other separate and independent documents or works, in or on a volume of a storage or distribution medium, is called an "aggregate" if the copyright resulting from the compilation is not used to limit the legal rights of the compilation's users beyond what the individual works permit. When the Document is included in an aggregate, this License does not apply to the other works in the aggregate which are not themselves derivative works of the Document.

If the Cover Text requirement of section 3 is applicable to these copies of the Document, then if the Document is less than one half of the entire aggregate, the Document's Cover Texts may be placed on covers that bracket the Document within the aggregate, or the electronic equivalent of covers if the Document is in electronic form. Otherwise they must appear on printed covers that bracket the whole aggregate.

Charles Manson

8. TRANSLATION

Translation is considered a kind of modification, so you may distribute translations of the Document under the terms of section 4. Replacing Invariant Sections with translations requires special permission from their copyright holders, but you may include translations of some or all Invariant Sections in addition to the original versions of these Invariant Sections. You may include a translation of this License, and all the license notices in the Document, and any Warranty Disclaimers, provided that you also include the original English version of this License and the original versions of those notices and disclaimers. In case of a disagreement between the translation and the original version of this License or a notice or disclaimer, the original version will prevail.

If a section in the Document is Entitled "Acknowledgements", "Dedications", or "History", the requirement (section 4) to Preserve its Title (section 1) will typically require changing the actual title.

9. TERMINATION

You may not copy, modify, sublicense, or distribute the Document except as expressly provided for under this License. Any other attempt to copy, modify, sublicense or distribute the Document is void, and will automatically terminate your rights under this License. However, parties who have received copies, or rights, from you under this License will not have their licenses terminated so long as such parties remain in full compliance.

10. FUTURE REVISIONS OF THIS LICENSE

The Free Software Foundation may publish new, revised versions of the GNU Free Documentation License from time to time. Such new versions will be similar in spirit to the present version, but may differ in detail to address new problems or concerns. See http://www.gnu.org/copyleft/.

Each version of the License is given a distinguishing version number. If the Document specifies that a particular numbered version of this License "or any later version" applies to it, you have the option of following the terms and conditions either of that specified version or of any later version that has been published (not as a draft) by the Free Software Foundation. If the Document does not specify a version number of this License, you may choose any version ever published (not as a draft) by the Free Software Foundation.

How to use this License for your documents

To use this License in a document you have written, include a copy of the License in the document and put the following copyright and license notices just after the title page:

Copyright (c) YEAR YOUR NAME.
Permission is granted to copy, distribute and/or modify this document under the terms of the GNU Free Documentation License, Version 1.2 or any later version published by the Free Software Foundation; with no Invariant Sections, no Front-Cover Texts, and no Back-Cover Texts. A copy of the license is included in the section entitled "GNU
Free Documentation License".

If you have Invariant Sections, Front-Cover Texts and Back-Cover Texts, replace the "with...Texts." line with this:

with the Invariant Sections being LIST THEIR TITLES, with the Front-Cover Texts being LIST, and with the Back-Cover Texts being LIST.

If you have Invariant Sections without Cover Texts, or some other combination of the three, merge those two alternatives to suit the situation.

If your document contains nontrivial examples of program code, we recommend releasing these examples in parallel under your choice of free software license, such as the GNU General Public License, to permit their use in free software.

Printed in the United States
206131BV00005B/282/P